Writers Who Changed the World

GEORGE ORWELL

Anita Croy

LUCENT
PRESS

Published in 2020 by
Lucent Press, an Imprint of Greenhaven Publishing, LLC
353 3rd Avenue
Suite 255
New York, NY 10010

Produced for Lucent by Calcium
Editors: Sarah Eason and Tim Cooke
Designers: Paul Myerscough and Lynne Lennon
Picture researcher: Rachel Blount

Picture credits: Cover: Shutterstock: Nikiteev_Konstantin; Inside: Shutterstock: 1000 Words: p. 31; Agsandrew: p. 32; Carlos Amarillo: p. 57; Andrey_Popov: p. 56; Thitsanu Angkapunyadech: p. 21b; Bissig: p. 34; BoxerX: p. 40; Valery Brozhinsky: pp. 22, 50; Casimiro PT: p. 51t; Oleksii Chumachenko: p. 42; Viktoriia Diachenko: p. 21t; Drop of Light: p. 55; Durantelallera: p. 30; Elzii: p. 39; Everett Historical: p. 37; Vic Hinterlang: p. 60; Igor Kisselev: p. 51b; Ktynzq: p. 44t; Masson: p. 38; Monster Ztudio: p. 59; M. Unal Ozmen: p. 49; AC Rider: pp. 9, 41t; Science Photo: p. 52; Sebos: p. 11; Elzbieta Sekowska: p. 27; Keith Tarrier: p. 28; Yenphoto24: p 61; Sonsedska Yuliia: p. 44b; Rudmer Zwerver: p. 29; Wellcome Collection: p. 48; Wikimedia Commons: Branch of the National Union of Journalists (BNUJ): p. 4; Eva Braun: p. 58; Adrian Cable: p. 8; Branson DeCou: p. 46; Evka W: p. 6; Eric Koch/Anefo: p. 35; Mikhail Koltsov: p. 10; Locospotter: p. 20; Ladislav Luppa: p. 12; Ministry of Information Photo Division Photographer: p. 25; The National Archives UK: p. 41bn; Tomas81j: p. 36; Unknown: pp. 15, 16, 17, 19c, 47; USAMHI: p. 19t; War Office official photographer, Console A (Captain): p. 7; Zilchy111 George Weir: p. 26.

Cataloging-in-Publication Data

Names: Croy, Anita.
Title: George Orwell / Anita Croy.
Description: New York : Lucent Press, 2020. | Series: Writers who changed the world | Includes glossary and index.
Identifiers: ISBN 9781534565906 (pbk.) | ISBN 9781534565913 (library bound) | ISBN 9781534565920 (ebook)
Subjects: LCSH: Orwell, George, 1903-1950--Juvenile literature. | Authors, English--20th century--Biography--Juvenile literature.
Classification: LCC PR6029.R8 C79 2020 | DDC 828'.91209 B--dc23

Printed in the United States of America

CPSIA compliance information: Batch #BS19KL: For further information contact Greenhaven Publishing LLC, New York, New York at 1-844-317-7404.

Please visit our website, www.greenhavenpublishing.com. For a free color catalog of all our high-quality books, call toll free 1-844-317-7404 or fax 1-844-317-7405.

CONTENTS

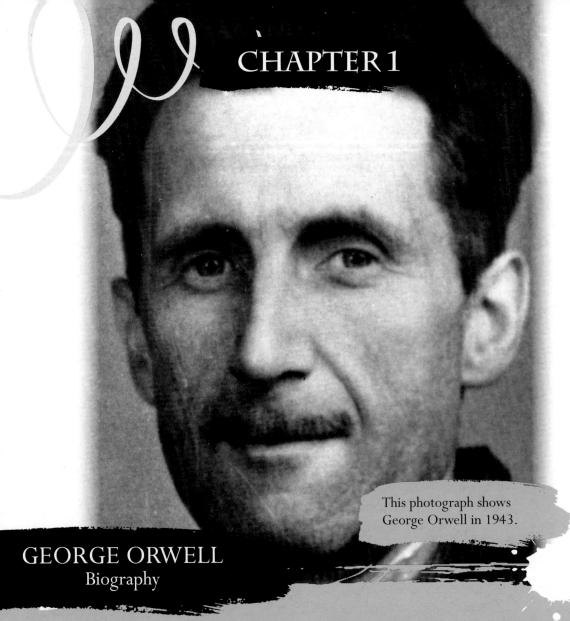

CHAPTER 1

This photograph shows George Orwell in 1943.

GEORGE ORWELL
Biography

Born: Eric Arthur Blair, June 25, 1903

Place of birth: Motihari, Bengal, India

Mother: Ida Mabel Limouzin

Father: Richard Walmesley Blair

Famous for: Writing two of the most visionary books in the English language, *Animal Farm* and *Nineteen Eighty-Four*.

How he changed the world: Orwell's view of an unfamiliar, unpleasant world has in many ways come true. Phrases he made up, such as "Thought Police," "Newspeak," and "doublethink," have entered everyday language.

George ORWELL'S vision of a state-controlled FUTURE has CHILLED modern-day readers with its ACCURACY.

George Orwell

A PRIVILEGED UPBRINGING

George Orwell was born Eric Blair in 1903 in India, where his father worked for the Indian Civil Service. When Eric was one year old, his mother took him and his older sister, Marjorie, back to England. He did not live with his father again until 1912.

Eton is one of England's most prestigious schools. It has produced many prime ministers and other leading individuals.

In 1917, Eric won a scholarship to the private boys' school, Eton. He was smart but lazy, and when he left school in 1921, he did not go to college. Instead, he decided to return to Asia. In 1922, he joined the Indian Imperial Police.

He was smart, but lazy …

Eric was sent to Burma (now Myanmar), where he was in charge of law enforcement for up to 200,000 people. He learned to speak Burmese fluently. He started to feel guilty about working for the British Empire. He felt the British had no right to rule Burma. In 1927, he quit his job to try writing for a living. He was also suffering from a chest infection. He would suffer from this illness throughout his life.

Words that changed the world

In Animal Farm, *the pigs who take over announce that all animals are "equal," but that some are "more equal than others."*

When World War II began, Orwell joined the Home Guard, which helped guard Great Britain against invasion.

Exploring the text

That some animals are more equal than others is one of the seven commandments, or rules, the animals must follow in Orwell's story, *Animal Farm*. The novella, or short novel, was a satire about communism in the Soviet Union. The book tells the story of how the animals take over Manor Farm to set up an ideal world. Instead, the pigs rule the other animals according to a system called Animalism. Orwell used Animalism to make fun of the rules of communism under the Soviet leader, Joseph Stalin.

Orwell believed Stalin had betrayed the Russian people. Under his leadership, nobody was allowed to disagree with him. Orwell's ideas were out of step with those of many Britons. In World War II (1939–1945), Stalin had been a valuable wartime ally of Great Britain and the United States.

HISTORY'S STORY

During the Spanish Civil War (1936–1939), Orwell went to Spain to fight against a military uprising. Orwell became suspicious of the influence of the Soviet Union on Spanish communists. He thought many people in Britain were deliberately ignoring the truth about Stalin. He was later proven right.

SYMPATHY WITH THE POOR

After George Orwell left the Indian Imperial Police in 1927, he decided to combine his desire to write for a living with his interest in improving the lives of the poor. He moved to London to find subjects to write about. There, Orwell relied on relatives and friends for food and places to stay. He walked around the East End of the city, which was a poor, run-down neighborhood. To make the experience more real, he dressed like a vagrant and lived in cheap lodging houses.

In 1928, Orwell moved to Paris, France, where his aunt lived. He spoke French fluently. For the next 18 months, he lived in a working-class neighborhood. He started writing novels, but his journalism proved more successful and he had a number of articles published in French and British newspapers. As in London, he dressed like a vagrant. He was fascinated by the hidden life that lay below the surface of the city—poverty and unemployment, and how they destroyed people's lives.

George Orwell took his pen name from the Orwell River, which flowed close to his parents' house in England.

Wigan Pier was a place on a canal where goods were unloaded and stored in the 1800s.

While in Paris, Orwell worked as a hotel dishwasher. He became seriously sick again, and he was also robbed. For Orwell, these were all important experiences. He believed that, in order to understand the poor, you had to be poor yourself.

Orwell's experiences in the two cities later appeared in his first book, *Down and Out in Paris and London* (1933). To save his parents from possible embarrassment, Eric Blair published the book under his pen name, George Orwell, which is how he became widely known.

The study of poverty

In 1929, Orwell had moved back to live with his parents in Suffolk, on England's east coast. The family home became his base for the next five years while he worked various jobs and wrote. Orwell's return home happened at the same time as the Wall Street Crash in New York City. This event started a collapse in the U.S. economy. It began a decade of global poverty and unemployment known as the Great Depression.

In 1936, Orwell was asked to write a book about the poverty of northern England. A friend recommended he visit Wigan in Lancashire. Orwell visited the city and the neighboring county of Yorkshire. The hardship he saw there formed his next book, *The Road to Wigan Pier* (1937). It was an account of the lives of working people, but its description of their struggles was very controversial.

A WRITER IN WARTIME

George Orwell had strong ideas of right and wrong, but he found his ideas tested by his time in Spain during the Spanish Civil War. A military officer named General Franco led an armed uprising to overthrow the government.
He was opposed by the Republicans. These were a mixure of Spanish socialists and communists. They were joined by volunteers from all over

This banner from the Spanish Civil War says "They shall not pass." It referred to Madrid's resistance to Franco's men.

Europe opposed to Franco's fascist rule, including Orwell and his new wife, Eileen O'Shaughnessy. Orwell served with a Republican unit until he was shot in the throat in May 1937. He survived, but then found his life threatened by Spanish communists. The communists were turning against other Republicans, whom they accused of working with Franco. Orwell and Eileen were lucky to escape to France.

World War II began in 1939. Orwell believed that the destruction and loss of life caused by World War I (1914–1918) were warnings against British involvement in a war in Europe. However, he believed the new war would become a power struggle between the ruling classes and ordinary British people. He therefore decided to support the government's declaration of war on Germany.

Helping the war effort

Orwell was unable to join the army because of his poor health, so he joined the Home Guard. This was a part-time army of 1.5 million volunteers who guarded the British coast and other important sites in cities and towns. They were trained to look out for signs of a German invasion.

Orwell also joined the British Broadcasting Corporation (BBC) in 1941. He worked for two years in the Eastern Service. His job was to write pro-British propaganda to be broadcast on the radio in India. Meanwhile, Eileen worked in the government's Censorship Department. Both jobs gave Orwell a valuable insight into how large bureaucratic organizations worked. Propaganda and censorhip would become important themes in *Nineteen Eighty-Four*.

Joseph Stalin took over the Soviet Union in 1924. He supported the Republicans in the Spanish Civil War.

Orwell resigned from the BBC in September 1943. He said that the articles he was writing for the BBC to broadcast were making no difference to the war effort. He believed that he could make more of an impact with his journalism and writing, and he wanted to spend more time on those things.

HISTORY'S STORY

In April 1936, Orwell's book *Keep the Aspidistra Flying* was published. An aspidistra is an indoor plant. The book, set in 1930s London, criticized people who put money above any other concern in life. Orwell wrote the book in 1934 and 1935, when he was living in London and working in a bookstore.

CHAPTER 2

This photograph shows Benito Mussolini (left) and Adolf Hitler.

EUROPE UNDER THE DICTATORS
Background

November 11, 1918: World War I comes to an end.

June 28, 1919: The Treaty of Versailles is signed, leaving Germany owing millions of dollars.

October 30, 1922: Benito Mussolini becomes the leader of Italy.

April 14, 1931: The Spanish monarchy is overthrown and a republic is set up.

January 30, 1933: Adolf Hitler is appointed chancellor of Germany.

July 17, 1936: Spanish Nationalists begin the Spanish Civil War.

March 30, 1939: The Spanish Civil War ends.

September 3, 1939: Britain and France declare war on Germany, beginning World War II.

Orwell's novels feature EXTREME CONTROL on the part of LEADERS, much like the control HITLER and MUSSOLINI exerted over people before and during WORLD WAR II.

RISE OF THE DICTATORS

When World War I ended in 1918, Europe's old order had changed forever. New political movements appeared to take the place of the traditional ruling classes. In Russia, communists seized control in a revolution in 1917. In Italy and Germany, nationalism, a belief in the importance of one's country, became the most powerful political force.

… Europe's old order had changed forever.

As Italian and German soldiers returned from the war, many were angry. Italy was on the winning side, but its economy was in ruins. The Germans believed their politicians had led them to defeat. Two men emerged who promised change. In Italy, a former reporter named Benito Mussolini started the Italian Fascist Party in 1912. He promised to restore Italian pride. In Germany, Adolf Hitler became leader of a small political party, the National Socialist German Workers' Party, or Nazis. He promised social change and a national revival. In Spain, General Francisco Franco fought against the republic that overthrew the Spanish king in 1936. After the end of the Spanish Civil War in 1939, Franco ruled Spain as a dictator until 1975.

Mussolini, Hitler, and Franco promised people that putting their trust in the nation could lead to a better future. Their vision attracted millions of followers. It also led directly to two conflicts: the Spanish Civil War and World War II.

Words that changed the world

In Homage to Catalonia, Orwell said that he had found it difficult to write about the Spanish war because there were so few documents about it that did not present only one side of the story. He said he had done his best to present an honest account, but inevitably, his view would have a bias.

Exploring the text

The text in *Homage to Catalonia* shows Orwell's concern in his war writings about how the truth was presented, because there were always two sides to every story. When he went to Spain to fight the fascists, he thought that the conflict was a straightforward struggle of right wing versus left wing. He was wrong. The war was far more complicated than this. As it continued, he found his communist colleagues began to fight other Republicans. The Spanish Civil War showed Orwell how complex the truth could be and how much propaganda had to do with "selling" one side or another of a story.

The Republican side in Spain started to fight among themselves, not just against Franco.

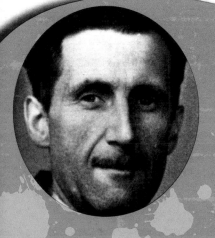

HISTORY'S STORY

Orwell's experience of fighting for the socialist cause in the Spanish Civil War was not a happy one. He was almost killed when a bullet hit him in the throat. Then the communists he supported turned against him. They said that he was working with the fascists.

15

TOTALITARIAN EUROPE

By the 1930s, Europe was in the grip of totalitarianism. This is a system of government in which everyone must obey the rules of the state. After World War I, many people believed democratic governments had proven too weak to be relied upon. They turned to Adolf Hitler, Benito Mussolini, and General Franco for strong leadership. In the communist Soviet Union, Joseph Stalin came to power in 1924. Like the fascist dictators, he had total control over the government.

Benito Mussolini took power in Italy when he became prime minister in 1922.

The dictators took complete control over how people lived their lives. To begin with, many of their citizens were happy with this arrangement. Totalitarian governments provided a sense of security and also hope for the future. They all shared some qualities. They only allowed one political party to exist, so there was no opposition. The party was ruled by a dictator. Individual rights were less important than the state, and every aspect of life was controlled. There was no free speech and the government used propaganda to reinforce its messages.

Creating totalitarian states

In the Soviet Union, Joseph Stalin set about strengthening his power. He used a secret police force to terrorize his opponents. In 1933, Stalin began the Great Purge. He got rid of all his rivals in the Communist Party. About 750,000 people were executed or sent to prison camps. Stalin launched a Five-Year Plan to improve Soviet industry. He placed all farms under state control, which led to a disastrous famine that killed millions of people.

In Italy, Benito Mussolini promised to restore Italy to the glory of the Roman Empire. He invaded Ethiopia in Africa in 1935 and Albania in 1939. At the same time, he took total power. In Germany, Adolf Hitler used propaganda to do well in elections. In 1933, he became chancellor of Germany. He ended democracy and took absolute power. He banned communism and turned on the Jewish people, whom he blamed for Germany's economic problems. He set out to restore German pride by invading neighboring Austria and Czechoslovakia (now Czech Republic).

Many people in the West admired Stalin for helping fight Hitler in World War II.

Orwell's version of Stalin's rise

In *Animal Farm*, Orwell tells the story of Stalin's rise to power. Manor Farm stands for Russia and the pig, Napoleon, is Joseph Stalin. The dogs are the secret police. The farmer, Mr. Jones, is the Russian ruler, who is overthrown. Orwell uses the story to show the horrors of Stalin's rule, which few people in Britain wanted to face.

A DIVIDED WORLD

When World War II ended in 1945, two countries dominated the globe: the United States and the Soviet Union. The two had different ideas about government and the economy. The United States favored individual freedom, democracy, and capitalism. The Soviet Union was a one-party communist state.

…two countries dominated …the United States and the Soviet Union.

At the end of the war, Soviet troops were positioned all over Eastern Europe, and the Soviet Union took control of the region. Germany was split into East and West Germany. The Soviet Union controlled the east of the country, including the eastern half of the former capital, Berlin. West Berlin was controlled by the United States, Great Britain, and France, who had fought together in the war. The whole of Europe was divided between the communist East and the democratic West. The British Prime Minister, Sir Winston Churchill, described the border between them as the "Iron Curtain."

The Cold War

As tensions rose between the East and West, a new phrase appeared: the Cold War. George Orwell had come up with the phrase in a piece of writing in 1945. By "Cold War," he meant that the United States and the Soviet Union were an ongoing threat to each other, but there was no direct military clash between them.

Words that changed the world

In Animal Farm, *Orwell describes how Napoleon sets up a committee of pigs to make decisions about the farm, without involving the other animals.*

Exploring the text

The new decision-making policy is brought in by Napoleon after he seizes power. The rest of the animals will now be ruled by laws made in secret by the pigs. Like Joseph Stalin in the Soviet Union, Napoleon is able to gain power because he has the backing of the dogs, which terrorize the other animals. In the same way, Stalin was able to rule as a dictator because the secret police who worked for him terrified the Soviet people.

U.S. and Soviet tanks face one another in Berlin during the Cold War.

The Soviets treated the hardest-working workers as heroes.

HISTORY'S STORY

In *Animal Farm*, Napoleon takes charge of the animals' production of eggs and milk. This echoes the way Stalin took control of all Soviet farms. In both the Soviet Union and on the farm, this led to famine. Later, Napoleon has his enemies killed because he fears they might take away his power. Similarly, Stalin had his enemies executed during his purges.

TIMELINE
1918–1945

1918   World War I ends.

1922   Benito Mussolini comes to power in Italy.
             George Orwell joins the Indian Imperial Police.

1928   George Orwell moves to Paris.

1929   The Great Depression begins.

1933   Adolf Hitler becomes chancellor of Germany.
             Down and Out in Paris and London is published.

1936   The Spanish Civil War begins.

1936   George Orwell and his wife Eileen go to Spain to
             support the Republicans.

Children in the Spanish
Civil War give the clenched
fist salute of the Republicans.

This square in Barcelona in Spain was named after Orwell to remember his fighting in the war.

1938 *Homage to Catalonia* is published.

1939 Russia and Germany agree not to fight each other.
World War II starts. George Orwell returns to England, and joins the Home Guard (1940).

1941 Germany invades the Soviet Union.
The United States joins the war.
Orwell joins the BBC.

1943 Orwell quits the BBC and the Home Guard. He becomes the editor of *Tribune* magazine.

1944 Orwell and Eileen adopt a son, Richard.

1945 World War II ends. The run-up to the Cold War intensifies.
Animal Farm is published.
Eileen dies suddenly.

At the end of World War II, Orwell had ideas about a world in which the government watched everyone.

CHAPTER 3

In the novel *Nineteen Eighty-Four*, everyone is watched by a ruler named Big Brother.

NINETEEN EIGHTY-FOUR
Masterwork

Written: 1947–1948

Where: Isle of Jura, Hebrides, Scotland

Published: June 1949

Publisher: Secker & Warburg, London

Working title: *The Last Man in Europe*

Translated into: 65 languages

Common terms invented by Orwell: Big Brother, Room 101, doublethink, Newspeak, Thought Police, thoughtcrime

The WORDS and TERMS that Orwell created in *Nineteen Eighty-Four* have become part of modern CULTURE, and are used regularly in discussions about STATE CONTROL and the MASS MEDIA.

INSPIRATIONS

In 1924, *We* by Yevgeny Zamyatin was published in English. Written in Russian, the novel told the story of a man living in a totalitarian state sometime in the near future. It described his attempts to rebel against the harsh rules of the unseen dictator who controls the state.

The plot is similar to that of George Orwell's *Nineteen Eighty-Four*. Orwell also told the story of a rebellious man living in a totalitarian state in the near future whose spirit is eventually broken by the authorities. Orwell had read Zamyatin's novel and written about it in an English newspaper, so it is likely that he was thinking about it when he started to write his own novel.

… the story of a rebellious man living in a totalitarian state …

A negative view

Real life events also influenced Orwell. Ever since the Spanish Civil War, he had been thinking about the relationship between the state, or government, and the individuals who lived in a country. Stalin's Soviet Union and the harsh way in which the Soviet state stamped out any individuality made Orwell worried about the future.

In addition, terrible events in his private life also made him deeply gloomy about the future. His London apartment was destroyed by a German flying bomb in June 1944. Less than a year later, in March 1945, his wife Eileen died unexpectedly following a hospital operation. She was just 39 years old.

Words that changed the world

In Nineteen Eighty-Four, *Winston tries to recall his childhood, but struggles. He asks where his memories went, and wonders if everything that he believes is his past is actually a lie, told by the Party.*

Exploring the text

Winston realizes that it is becoming harder to remember the past clearly, because he has nothing to help him except his own memory. The Party, which controls every aspect of people's lives, controls memories, too. It wants to replace people's memories with its own version of the past. In this way it makes a new "truth"—the Party's truth, not Winston's, even about his own mother.

These rescue workers are looking for survivors in a bombed house in London during World War II.

HISTORY'S STORY

In late 1943, U.S. President Franklin D. Roosevelt, British Prime Minister Winston Churchill, and Soviet leader Joseph Stalin met in Tehran in Iran. The leaders decided their next steps in the war against Germany. Orwell believed that they agreed to divide the postwar world into three superstates once Germany lost the war. The three superstates in his novel echo this division.

25

WRITING
NINETEEN EIGHTY-FOUR

Eileen died suddenly in March 1945. George Orwell was now the only parent of his young son Richard, whom he and Eileen had adopted the previous year. Life in London was tough. Orwell worked as a journalist night and day to help cope with his grief. *Animal Farm* had just been published, and its success meant Orwell was in great demand.

Unable to deal with the pressure, Orwell turned for help to his friend and editor at *The Observer* newspaper, David Astor. Astor's family owned a farm on the Scottish island of Jura in the Hebrides, and he offered to let Orwell live there. In May 1946, Orwell made the long train and boat journey to the island. Free from the need to write for newspapers and magazines, Orwell had the time to work on his novel, which he planned to title *The Last Man in Europe*. The house was so far from anywhere that he had to take as many supplies with him as possible. He wrote his friend, the novelist Arthur Koestler, that getting ready was "almost like stocking up ship for an Arctic voyage."

This photograph shows Barnhill, the farmhouse on Jura where Orwell wrote the book. It is still in use.

A hard winter

The winter of 1946 was one of the coldest on record, and Orwell was not in good health. The house had no electricity, so Orwell burned peat, a soil-like material dug from the ground, to keep warm. He used a small gas burner to cook on and paraffin lamps for light. During the day, he worked on his novel. At the end of the freezing winter, Orwell was joined by his sister Avril, who also brought Richard. Writing went well. By May 1947, Orwell had finished almost a third of his novel. Then disaster struck.

Orwell used lamps such as this one for reading and writing on the long, dark winter evenings on Jura.

On a lovely day in August, Orwell, Avril, Richard, and some friends almost drowned. They were sailing on the sea when their boat turned over, plunging them into the freezing water. Orwell had suffered for years from weak lungs, but now the combination of hard work and getting cold in the water led to him becoming seriously sick. In November 1947, he learned he had tuberculosis, or TB, a possibly fatal lung condition.

Race against time

Orwell grew weaker, but he was determined to get on with finishing *Nineteen Eighty-Four*. He tried an experimental drug from the United States, which cured the TB after three months. However, it left him with terrible side effects. Instead of taking time to recover fully, Orwell started writing again in spring 1948. His publisher wanted the book to come out as soon as possible. By the time he delivered the book in December 1948, Orwell was terminally ill.

PLOT BREAKDOWN

Nineteen Eighty-Four is set 40 years after the end of World War II, when the United States dropped atom bombs on Japan. The future that Orwell describes is unrecognizable. The main character, Winston Smith, lives in Oceania, one of three superstates that survived the so-called Atomic Wars.

Everything in Oceania is controlled by the state's secret police. Every house is monitored, and every activity and conversation is watched. People are no longer free to do as they wish. Everything must be done according to the orders of the state. Watching over the people is Big Brother, the leader of the Party, who seems to be everywhere.

A dangerous love story

Winston works as a low-ranking official in the ruling party in the capital (it is based on London). He dreams of rebelling against the Party and the state. He falls in love with Julia, another Party worker. By falling in love, they are breaking Party rules. They meet in secret.

In the novel, the world is in a constant war as the three superstates fight one another.

The Party makes everyone scared of everyone else, because nobody knows whom they can trust—if anyone. Distracted by his love affair, Winston foolishly places his trust in several people who turn out to be secret police or members of the Party. The state finally sends Winston for "reeducation." Tortured and made to face his greatest fear (rats), he gives in and agrees to follow the Party. He betrays Julia and transfers his love to Big Brother.

Rats are a symbol of how Winston is trapped in a cage.

A nightmare world

One of the most disturbing ideas in *Nineteen-Eighty Four* is the Thought Police. They get inside people's heads to find out what they are thinking. Crimes are committed just by being thought of. The state rewrites history to its own benefit so that the truth no longer exists. Big Brother himself might or might not exist—the reader never finds out—but even imagining him is enough to terrify people. In Orwell's nightmare world, people are tortured in Room 101. There, the Thought Police ensure that each individual is tortured by whatever thing terrifies them most. In this way, they are "reeducated" to love the Party.

HISTORY'S STORY

Orwell intended *Nineteen Eighty-Four* to be a satire on totalitarian rule. The novel takes the idea of totalitarianism to an extreme to show what might happen if such governments are allowed to take control. He invents a new language to show a state dominated by fear. Orwell imagines a totalitarian future as a place where a human face is stamped on by a boot—forever.

MAIN CHARACTERS

Winston Smith

The 39-year-old worker is at the heart of the novel. He works for the Ministry of Truth, where he rewrites the records of the past. Winston (whom Orwell may or may not have named for Great Britain's wartime prime minister, Sir Winston Churchill) rebels against the Party, falls in love with Julia, and writes a diary. Eventually this behavior leads to his arrest. At first, he stands up to the Party, but after he is tortured he gives in and becomes a Party follower.

Big Brother's image is everywhere in Oceania.

Julia

We never learn Julia's last name. She is 26 years old and works in the Fiction Department. Winston suspects her at first of being a spy, and we never really learn if she is or not. Winston eventually gives her up to the Party when he is tortured.

O'Brien

O'Brien is a member of the Inner Party. Winston trusts him and thinks O'Brien will understand his objections to the Party. In fact, O'Brien is a fanatical Party supporter whose job it is to convert people to the Party's beliefs.

Big Brother

The leader of the Party may or may not be an actual person, but he appears on images throughout Oceania and is referred to constantly throughout *Nineteen Eighty-Four*. His eyes follow the citizens constantly.

This poster is for a play based on *Nineteen Eighty-Four*.

Mr. Charrington

He runs a secondhand store and rents a room to Winston where he and Julia can meet. Winston trusts him, but Charrington is actually a member of the Thought Police.

Syme

Syme works with Winston at the Ministry of Truth.

Parsons

Parsons is a Party member who works at the Ministry of Truth and lives near Winston. His children are junior spies.

CHAPTER 4

The Thought Police have ways of reading people's minds.

NINETEEN EIGHTY-FOUR
Key Themes

Nineteen Eighty-Four's major themes include:

The dangers of totalitarianism

Technology's growing power

The importance of language and meaning in thought and politics

Conflict between the individual and the social system

Power and powerlessness

Love and loyalty

Thought control

Orwell's themes of TOTALITARIANISM, the systematic USE of language to CONTROL people, and the POWER of TECHNOLOGY are especially MEANINGFUL today in our world of HIGH-TECH computers and SOCIAL NETWORKING.

TOTALITARIANISM

In *Nineteen Eighty-Four*, George Orwell set out to show his reader an extreme kind of totalitarian government. In the novel, the state has complete power. It controls every detail of every part of every citizen's life. It is even able to punish thoughts that break Party rules, because it has the technology to understand what people are thinking.

Joseph Stalin's type of communism is often described as Stalinism.

Orwell's suspicion of Stalin's Soviet state and his experiences during the Spanish Civil War had convinced him that communism was a great evil. He believed the communist state would destroy the freedom of its citizens to protect its own interests. In this, Orwell was going against popular public opinion of the day. The Soviet Union had helped the Allies defeat Germany. Newspapers in the United States and Europe praised the Soviet Union. They said the communist state was a brave social experiment. They praised Stalin as a strong leader. It was not until later that the full horrors of living in Stalin's Soviet state became clear.

In the novel, the state has complete power.

In Orwell's novel, Winston Smith tries to go against the system through an act of rebellion—having a relationship with Julia. By the end of the novel, any thought of rebellion is destroyed. The power of the state is greater than he could have imagined, and Winston becomes its slave.

Words that changed the world

In Nineteen Eighty-Four, *Orwell writes that the "black mustachioed face" of Big Brother gazes down at people almost everywhere. The message is powerful—Big Brother is watching you, wherever you are.*

Exploring the text

A totalitarian state aims to show its subjects that it has complete power by demonstrating that it controls every part of life. The posters of Big Brother's face, with its piercing eyes, are plastered all over the city to remind people that they are being watched all the time. Big Brother never appears in the book. He is referred to constantly as the leader of Oceania, the totalitarian state in which Winston Smith lives. Nobody knows for sure if Big Brother really exists, but his image and the constant reminders that "Big Brother is watching you" are typical of the way a totalitarian state controls its citizens.

Like George Orwell, Arthur Koestler took part in the Spanish Civil War.

HISTORY'S STORY

Orwell was close friends with the British-Hungarian novelist Arthur Koestler. Initially, Koestler supported Stalin, but he soon grew worried about the Soviet state. In 1940, he published *Darkness at Noon*. In the novel, a Soviet man is eventually convinced to plead guilty to crimes he did not commit.

THOUGHT CONTROL

Propaganda is one of the main ways the Party controls its citizens. As part of its propaganda, language is an important tool of thought control. The Party uses a language called Newspeak, which controls people by limiting the words that they are allowed to use. Newspeak does not include words that describe rebellion or freedom of thought. The Party argues that if the words do not exist, rebellion and freedom of thought do not exist.

The Party also uses its control of language to control the past. It removes words linked with the past from the language, so citizens can no longer talk about the past and it becomes less important. The Party's ultimate aim is to remove citizens' ability to have any anti-Party thoughts by trapping them in the present, where the Party is in control.

Stalin began an official newspaper called *Pravda*, or "Truth." In reality, it contained little that was true.

Ministry of Truth

As well as limiting language, the Party also controls all information that is released to the public. This is part of Winston Smith's job in the Ministry of Truth.

The Ministry is responsible for all the Party's publications and information. Every fact and figure is made up by the Party to fit its latest ideas. The Ministry corrects old information when the Party changes its position on subjects such as food or which other state is the enemy. According to O'Brien, a member of the Inner Party, the Party decides what is and is not true.

States such as Nazi Germany used military order to control their citizens.

Forms of propaganda

The Party has constructed different forms of propaganda in order to fill all citizens' daily lives, so they will have no time to think about rebellion. The propaganda tries not only to get citizens to obey Party orders but also to hate anything that is not the Party. Each day, there is a Two Minute Hate, when Party members must watch a film of the Party's enemies. During Hate Week, everyone must spend the week directing their hatred toward the Party's latest enemy. Each morning at 7:18 a.m., every citizen has to do a fitness workout while following the telescreen, or interactive TV, in their room. Posters of Big Brother are everywhere to underline the idea that every citizen is continually being watched.

In illustrating these different forms of Party control in his novel, Orwell is giving the reader a warning. He shows how propaganda can be used to control information so that it becomes impossible to say whether anything is true or even real. The whole state of Oceania only exists as the Party decides to define it.

LOVE AND LOYALTY

The Party sets out to create hatred and fear in Oceania, so there is no room for love. The Party wants to get rid of any love apart from love for Big Brother and the Party. Winston himself sees how it is working to destroy people's love for their families.

One of Winston's most precious memories is of how his mother showered love on him and his sister and tried to protect them. By contrast, the Party destroys the bonds between parents and children in the Parsons family. The Parsons children belong to the Junior Spies. Their first loyalty is to the Party, not their parents.

Unquestioning loyalty

Winston's act of rebellion against the Party is to fall in love with Julia. His love is eventually destroyed, however. O'Brien tortures him and forces him to give Julia up and swear his love and loyalty to the Party.

The love affair between Winston and Julia lasts only a few months.

The Party can only survive if all its citizens remain loyal. It uses fear to force its citizens to support everything it does. The ultimate aim of the Party is to make every citizen unhesitatingly loyal. In Oceania, personal feelings must always come second to loyalty to the Party. Winston is unusual because he manages to remain loyal to both Julia and the Party until the end of the book.

A fight for loyalty

At the heart of *Nineteen Eighty-Four* is the struggle between O'Brien and Winston for Winston's loyalty. After Winston is arrested, O'Brien first uses torture and drugs to try to force him to give up Julia and show his devotion to the Party. Winston convinces O'Brien he has done this, but wakes up after a nightmare shouting his love for Julia. Winston assumes he will be executed, but O'Brien decides that the way to force him to be loyal to the Party is to send him to Room 101. There, Winston is terrified into giving up the woman he loves, shouting, "Do it to Julia!"

O'Brien threatens to let rats eat Winston's face.

HISTORY'S STORY

Room 101 contains the greatest fear of whomever is sent there. For Winston, this is rats. When a cage of rats is attached to his face, he finally screams for it to be attached to Julia instead. O'Brien has broken him. As the novel ends, Winston realizes that "He loved Big Brother."

ORWELL'S MAJOR NOVELS AND THEIR THEMES

Down and Out in Paris and London (1933)

This is a nonfiction book about living in two major cities with no money. In Paris, Orwell works in a hotel kitchen. In London, he lives as a vagrant, staying in cheap hostels.

Keep the Aspidistra Flying (1936)

The novel's hero, George Comstock, decides to live without joining the common worship of money, but this only causes him misery.

The Road to Wigan Pier (1937)

This is an investigation of the lives of the poor in northern England. The book also explains Orwell's own socialist beliefs but says that most of the poor are opposed to the idea of socialism.

Aspidistras were popular house plants.

Once a busy port, Wigan was poor by the 1930s.

Homage to Catalonia (1938)

This is Orwell's account of the Spanish Civil War. It explains why Orwell does not trust communism.

Coming Up for Air (1939)

In this novel, Orwell remembers his childhood and writes about the war he feels is about to begin.

Animal Farm (1945)

This is a satire on Joseph Stalin's Soviet Union, acted out by animals on an English farm.

Nineteen Eighty-Four (1949)

A novel that predicts the immediate future if totalitarianism is allowed to take hold.

This illustration shows a scene from *Animal Farm*.

CHAPTER 5

These people are Nationalist protestors in Ukraine.

A WARNING
Effecting Change

George Orwell's warnings:

In *Nineteen Eighty-Four*, Orwell warned us about a world that might exist if people did not guard the right to freedom of thought. Many people see the book as predicting elements of the world in which we live:

The rise of nationalism: In many European countries, nationalist political parties are growing more popular, with their belief in loyalty to the state and dislike of foreigners.

The rise of populism: Politicians have emerged in many countries who back the power of the people over the power of the elite. They often choose popular policies over wise policies.

The rise of social media: Technology such as computers and the Internet have put much of people's lives on display, especially through the use of social media.

Many people today view Orwell's writing as a STARTLING PREDICTION of the FUTURE. They claim that we see all of Orwell's FICTIONAL THEMES becoming REALITY today in the form of NATIONALISM, POPULISM, and the rise of technological control through SOCIAL MEDIA.

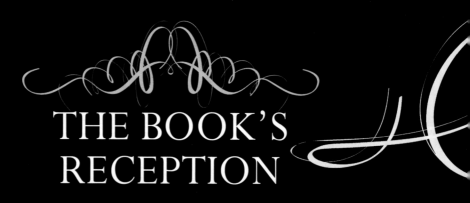

THE BOOK'S RECEPTION

Orwell's last novel, *Nineteen Eighty-Four* was an instant best seller when it appeared in 1949 in both Great Britain and the United States. It sold hundreds of thousands of copies in America after it was chosen by the Book-of-the-Month Club and *Reader's Digest*, which both had many members and readers. In Great Britain, the book sold 50,000 copies in the first year, despite the poverty that remained after the end of World War II.

The book appeared at a time when tensions between the West and the Soviet Union were increasing. It helped make it easier to understand the abstract idea of a totalitarian state and what it meant to the people who lived there. The horrors of Room 101, for example, showed the reader what happened when a person no longer was allowed to think or speak for themselves. Similarly, the idea that a "Big Brother" could watch a person's every move helped those in the West understand what it might be like to live in a state where the secret police monitored everyone.

… tensions between the West and the Soviet Union were increasing.

Some critics thought that Orwell went too far. The novel was set in the not-too-distant future, but they thought the world it described was nothing like the world as it existed. They claimed that is was so far removed from reality that it was impossible. This was partly because many of Orwell's readers still believed Joseph Stalin was a skilled leader of the Soviet Union and not the brutal man he was later shown to be.

Words that changed the world

In the conclusion of Animal Farm, *the faces of the pigs dramatically change—from animal to human. Orwell writes that the other farm animals look at the pigs and see that they have become humanlike. It is now impossible to tell what is a pig and what is a human.*

Exploring the text

In the final sentences of *Animal Farm*, the pigs who led the animals to break free of the control of humans have now become just like humans. When they persuaded the other animals to rebel against Mr. Jones, the farmer, the pigs promised their new lives would be freer and happier. Over the course of the novella, it becomes clear that the pigs have no intention of sharing their authority with the other animals. Instead, the pigs have worked their way into a position of power where they rule over the other animals using fear and bullying. For the other animals, conditions under the pigs are far worse than life had been under Mr. Jones. The other animals have been taken in and used by the pigs—just as Orwell believed the Russians had been taken in by Joseph Stalin.

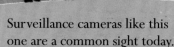

Surveillance cameras like this one are a common sight today.

Animal Farm suggests that those who rebel against their oppressors may eventually turn into oppressors themselves.

QUESTIONING TOTALITARIANISM

During and immediately after the end of World War II, Joseph Stalin was praised not just by the leaders of the West but also by ordinary people. He had helped the Allies stand up to Adolf Hitler's Nazis. People were reluctant to see Stalin as anything other than a friend of the West. In the Soviet Union, however, Stalin's rule had been difficult for many Russians for decades.

In 1928, Stalin ordered the seizure of private farms to create large farms run by the government. He wanted to control every aspect of Russian life, from its economy to its society. Many left-wing thinkers in the West applauded his plan, but within several years it was clear that it had failed. By 1938, more than 90 percent of all farmers worked on collective farms, but a series of crop failures led to mass starvation. This was hidden from the West.

This is a monument to Stalin's Five-Year Plan to improve industry—by making workers work harder.

Getting rid of enemies

In 1937, Stalin launched the Great Purge. He first killed or imprisoned all his political enemies within the Communist Party. He then got rid of anyone who disagreed with him, including some artists and scientists. He controlled every aspect of people's lives through the secret police and used the media to spread propaganda. He controlled what was taught in schools. People were no longer allowed to be creative. Religion was outlawed. Those who disobeyed the rules were executed.

Unlike many other left-wing thinkers and journalists in the West, George Orwell was suspicious of Stalin. He came to believe long before other people that the Russian leader was a dictator. Both *Animal Farm* and *Nineteen Eighty-Four* were fictional criticisms of the Soviet state under Stalin. In *Animal Farm*, Orwell used the pigs' takeover of the farm to show what had happened in Russia under Stalin. In *Nineteen Eighty-Four*, he takes his fiction a step further to show how a totalitarian state might look if Stalin were allowed to continue without being stopped.

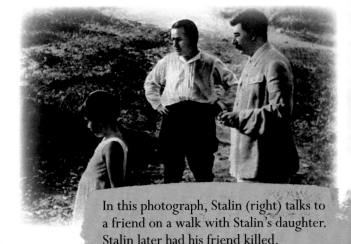

In this photograph, Stalin (right) talks to a friend on a walk with Stalin's daughter. Stalin later had his friend killed.

HISTORY'S STORY

Orwell set out to make his totalitarian state as real as possible. In Oceania, as in Soviet Russia, nobody is allowed to be creative or to think for themselves. Everything must be done for the greater good of the state. Many of the ideas Orwell created were so powerful they are still used as a shorthand for government control over the individual.

ORWELL'S LAST YEARS

Writing *Nineteen Eighty-Four* killed George Orwell. He was already in poor health when he moved to Jura in the Hebrides to write the novel. Following the boating accident that left him awaiting rescue in the freezing waters of the North Sea, his health got much worse. He caught the lung disease TB, which was often fatal.

TB patients were put in hospitals called sanatoriums, where they rested in the hope they would recover.

Under pressure from his publisher, Orwell continued to write the book while he spent seven months recovering in a hospital near Glasgow, Scotland. He even delayed going to a sanatorium in southern England because he wanted to get the book finished. He made the final changes to the text while he was in the sanatorium. The book was published on June 8, 1949.

By then, it was clear that Orwell's sickness would kill him. He spent his last few months in the hospital in London, where he married his second wife, Sonia Brownell, in October. He never left his hospital room.

George Orwell died alone on January 21, 1950, at the age of 46 in University College Hospital. His sister Avril and son Richard were still living in the cottage on Jura when they heard the news on the radio.

Orwell gave his readers instructions on how to make strong tea using the equivalent of 10 tea bags!

A famous journalist

During his lifetime, Orwell was almost as famous as a reporter as for his novels. On March 29, 1940, he wrote his first piece for *Tribune*, a socialist magazine that appeared every two weeks. In 1943, Orwell became its literary editor, and wrote reviews of books. He also wrote articles under the title "As I Please," which gave his views on subjects ranging from the atom bomb to how to make the perfect cup of tea.

Early in 1945, Orwell become a war correspondent for *The Observer*, a leading Sunday newspaper. The paper had tried to hire him in 1943, but he had failed the medical exam. In 1945, he somehow got the job. He moved to Paris, France, from where he traveled around Europe to report on World War II.

HISTORY'S STORY

Orwell spent many years working as a journalist to support himself and his family. He worked for many magazines and newspapers, writing reviews of plays, books, and movies. He also wrote political pieces and essays for publications that had more socialist ideas.

ORWELL'S PHRASES

Many of George Orwell's most famous phrases have entered the English language as a kind of shorthand.

Big Brother

The idea that everyone is being watched at all times and in all places. The phrase gave its name to a TV show.

Newspeak

A language with limited words in order to keep people from having too many thoughts. It is used in all the Party's propaganda.

Doublethink

The ability to have two separate thoughts that cancel each other out but to think them both true.

Big Brother's eyes seem to follow people from posters on the wall.

Many people believe that politicians use doublethink to switch between beliefs.

relevant but is really
politicians.
doublethink noun
stance of, two oppo
by George Orwell

Thought Police/Thoughtcrime

In Oceania, the police are able to access people's thoughts. Thinking against the Party is a crime.

Room 101

A prison room in which people's worst fears come true. The phrase is used as the title of a British TV show where celebrities discuss things they hate.

Unperson

After a person is executed, all traces of them are removed and they become an unperson, as if they had never existed.

The Party uses the Thought Police to silence criticism before it can even be spoken aloud.

CHAPTER 6

Today, cameras watch us all the time.

ORWELL'S LEGACY
Aftermath

Orwell's predictions that have come true:

Big Brother is watching you: Today, surveillance cameras are part of everyday life.

Telescreens: Thanks to social media, everything we do and then post online is logged and recorded forever.

Doublethink: Many politicians often seem to claim to believe two opposite things at the same time.

Facecrime: The idea that someone's expression can show that they are guilty of thoughtcrime is similar to the judgment of people on social media from almost no information.

Look at the WORLD around you—can you RECOGNIZE any of the following of Orwell's IDEAS in your LIFE: Big Brother, telescreens, doublethink, and facecrime?

SETTING THE AGENDA

The central theme of *Nineteen Eighty-Four* is the conflict between the individual and the social system in which he or she lives. George Orwell imagines a near-future world in which Winston Smith's personality is broken by a system that exists not for the benefit of its citizens but solely for the benefit of the state.

> *... Winston Smith's personality is broken by a system that exists ... for the benefit of the state.*

Like other socialists, Orwell believed government needed to play a role in daily life. *Nineteen Eighty-Four*, however, was a warning about what happened when this government involvement is taken to extremes. Orwell had seen totalitarian states emerge in Hitler's Germany and Stalin's Russia. Since World War II, there have been others, such as Iraq, which was ruled by Saddam Hussein from 1979 until 2003.

Orwell also anticipated a future in which the truth would be able to be changed. The idea of "fake news" became an important issue after the election of Donald Trump as president of the United States in late 2016. Trump labeled any criticism of him as "fake news." This raised questions about how we know what is the truth. If somebody repeats many times that something is true, does that make it true? In *Nineteen Eighty-Four,* one of the Party's most important propaganda weapons is its ability to rewrite history to suit its needs.

Words that changed the world

In Nineteen Eighty-Four, *Winston writes that the Party had said a person must no longer believe what their eyes and ears show them. Yet, Winston says he believes that the solid world around him is real and there are undeniable facts such as* "stones are hard, water is wet." *Winston believes that these things that he sees and feels are true, despite what the Party says.*

Exploring the text

In this part of the novel, Winston is writing in his diary. This is an illegal activity for which he could be put to death. He writes that the way people know if something is real or not comes from the evidence of our senses. His biggest fear is that the Party is able to control all of its citizens' senses, so it is able to change reality to suit its own needs. For Winston, the issue is complicated further because he finds it hard to separate his memories from what he sees and hears. This means that he is not sure if he can completely trust his own thoughts. He decides to put his faith in O'Brien, who he thinks will be able to show him what is really "real," but his decision is mistaken and has terrible consequences.

As president, Donald Trump has often been caught saying things that are not true, but has also been known to call criticisms of him "fake news."

WHO'S WATCHING YOU?

One of the scariest aspects of *Nineteen Eighty-Four* is that individuals are never alone. They are watched everywhere by the telescreens. The telescreens are sensitive enough to detect changes in facial expression. In every street, a picture of Big Brother stares down at them. The Thought Police punish anyone who has ideas that are not approved by the Party.

When the novel was published in 1949, few people could imagine a world in which thoughts and actions are monitored. Fewer than 70 years later, however, Orwell's fears have come true. The idea of 24-hour-a-day surveillance has been a reality for decades. From cameras that record our movements in the street or inside stores to cell phones and computers that store data about our locations, nearly every move people make is being monitored and watched.

In the past, the government sometimes monitored individuals, such as criminals. They might have their mail read or their phone calls listened to. Today, technology makes it possible for organizations such as the National Security Agency (NSA) in the United States to secretly read millions of emails and listen to what millions of citizens are saying on phone calls.

In hotels and apartment buildings, the halls are often constantly monitored.

The TV show *Big Brother* was first described as a kind of scientific experiment, but over time it became popular entertainment.

Big Brother at work

Today, the idea that Big Brother is watching all of us is very common. The idea even inspired a reality TV show, *Big Brother*. Created in 1997 in Holland, the show put a number of contestants in a house and isolated them from the outside world. Cameras and microphones recorded their every move as they were constantly under surveillance. Each week, the public got to vote off their least favorite contestant, and the last person left won $500,000. In 1998, the U.S. movie *The Truman Show* told the story of a man whose whole life is screened on TV. Everyone else in his life is an actor, and where he lives is a huge movie set. Cameras follow him everywhere. In many ways, the idea that people are watched all the time is no longer considered unusual.

HISTORY'S STORY

Thanks to social media such as Facebook, Instagram, and Snapchat, many people now invite others to watch all parts of their lives. This goes against Orwell's warnings about protecting individual freedoms. However, many people are bullied or criticized online. Social media is seen by some people as being negative as well as positive.

FIGHTING THE DICTATORS

George Orwell lived during and took part in two terrible wars, the Spanish Civil War and World War II. He saw dictators in Spain, Germany, and Italy take over their countries, and the damage their nationalist beliefs did when they led Europe into conflict. He also saw great changes in the Soviet Union. After the Russian Revolution in 1917, many people hoped the new communist country would be a place where there was no poverty and where everyone was treated equally. Instead, Orwell realized, Joseph Stalin turned it into a totalitarian state.

This photograph shows Mussolini and Hitler. They worked together to try to spread fascism throughout Europe.

The leaders of Germany and Italy, Adolf Hitler and Benito Mussolini, promised their followers that they would make things better for them after the devastation of World War I. In both countries, the men became dictators. It soon became clear that anybody who disagreed with either leader risked being executed.

Both leaders set out to create societies in which everyone shared their views. Those who did not were imprisoned or killed. Stalin, Hitler, and Mussolini all ruled by using fear to make sure that people followed their orders.

A delayed prediction

Orwell wanted to warn his readers what might happen if people allowed their freedom and rights to be eroded. Many parts of his vision of the future have come true, although in fact he was ahead of his time. Orwell chose the year 1984 by simply reversing the numbers of the year when he was writing, 1948. When 1984 came around, the world had not changed quite as he predicted. Computer technology was in its early days, and people had yet to understand the power of the Internet. Surveillance cameras and cell phones were still rare. That was all about to change. As we now know, if Orwell had titled his book *Two Thousand and Four*, many of his predictions would have become true by then!

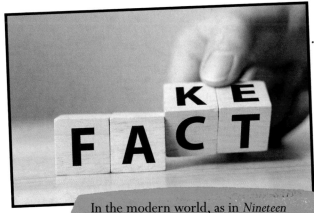

In the modern world, as in *Nineteen Eighty-Four*, the line between fact and fiction is often blurred.

HISTORY'S STORY

Thanks to George Orwell, many people saw the year 1984 as a special date when it arrived. Many of Orwell's predictions had not yet been realized, but the power of Orwell's imagination was enough to make people aware of the significance of the year. In fact, it would be another two decades before Orwell's world came closer to life.

VISIONS OF AN UNPLEASANT FUTURE

Nineteen Eighty-Four is just one of many novels that have looked forward to a dystopian future, or a future that is worse than the present.

The Time Machine (1895), H.G. Wells

In this novel, a Victorian traveler visits the year 802,701. He finds that humanity has split into two races, the childlike Eloi and the dangerous and threatening Morlocks.

Brave New World (1932), Aldous Huxley

Huxley's novel takes place in a future in which the world is all a single state that people are made to believe is perfect. The story tells how one man challenges this idea.

Women wearing costumes from Margaret Atwood's novel *The Handmaid's Tale*

Book burning is at the heart of *Fahrenheit 451*.

Fahrenheit 451 (1953), Ray Bradbury

In Bradbury's future version of the United States, all books are banned and any that are found are burned by government employees called firemen. The title is a reference to the temperature at which paper burns. One fireman, Montag, quits and joins a secret group that tries to remember and share all the world's greatest books.

A Clockwork Orange (1962), Anthony Burgess

This novel is set in a future England governed by a totalitarian state. It tells the story of violent and destructive teenage criminals, who speak their own language based on Russian. The gang's leader, Alex, is caught and put in prison, forcing him to think about giving up his life of crime.

The Handmaid's Tale (1985), Margaret Atwood

The Canadian author describes a United States that has been taken over by a totalitarian religious government that sets up a state called Gilead. Fewer women are able to have babies, so those who can are forced to become "handmaids" and have babies on behalf of the leaders of the state. The novel describes the attempts of the handmaid Offred to become free.

GLOSSARY

absolute power government with a ruler whose orders cannot be questioned

Allies the countries that fought Germany and Japan in World War II, led by the United States, Great Britain, and the Soviet Union

ally someone who works with someone else to achieve something

atom bombs weapons that release energy contained in tiny particles called atoms

authorities people or groups who have control over a system

betrayed gave damaging evidence about someone

bias unfair favoring of one side over another

bureaucratic belonging to a large organization of officials

capitalism an economic system in which owners run businesses for profit

censorship the banning of information or works that support unwelcome ideas

civil service the people who carry out the activities of a government

class a system of organizing people according to their place in society, such as working class or middle class

collective carried out by everyone together

communists people who believe the government should own everything and share it among everyone

controversial causing disagreement

democratic related to a political system in which citizens vote for their government

dictator a ruler who personally lays down the laws of a country

economy the business, industry, and trade of a country

editor someone who prepares a newspaper or magazine to be published

elite a small group of people at the top of society

executed killed by the government

famine a shortage of food that causes deaths

fascist describes a style of government by dictators with military-style discipline

fluently easily, without hesitation

Great Depression a period of low economic activity and global poverty in the 1930s

grief great sorrow, especially at someone's death

imperial related to an empire

infection a disease that can be passed on

left wing having a point of view that may include socialist or communist beliefs

loyalty strong support for another person

media newspapers, TV, and radio stations

monitored closely watched

mustachioed having a mustache

nonfiction writing about real subjects

paraffin a type of wax that burns

pen name a made-up name under which an author writes books

policy a course of action

poverty severe financial harship

propaganda material intended to persuade people to support or oppose a particular idea

purge getting rid of something

rebel to turn against authority

Republicans in the Spanish Civil War, those fighting to defend the Spanish republic

revolution the violent overthrow of a ruler

right wing believing in strict and traditional forms of government

satire a work that makes fun of something

scholarship a sum of money to help students

shorthand a short, simple way to refer to something

side effects unwelcome effects of taking medical drugs

slogan a memorable phrase

socialists people who believe major industries should be owned and controlled by the government, rather than individuals

superstates states formed from many countries

surveillance close observation of someone

terminally in a way that will end in death

terrorize to deliberately frighten people

tortured made to feel severe pain

uprising a rebellion against a government

vagrant someone who lives by begging

visionary someone who imagines something new or different

volunteers people who freely offer to do something

FOR MORE INFORMATION

BOOKS

Boon, Kevin Alexander. *George Orwell: Animal Farm and Nineteen Eighty-Four*. New York, NY: Marshall Cavendish Benchmark, 2009.

Cernak, Linda. *Joseph Stalin: Dictator of the Soviet Union*. Minneapolis, MN: Essential Library, 2016.

Orwell, George. *Animal Farm*. New York, NY: Penguin Classics, 2018.

Orwell, George. *Nineteen Eighty-Four*. New York, NY: Penguin Classics, 2018.

WEBSITES

Dictators—people.howstuffworks.com/dictator1.htm
This website includes a history of dictatorship and totalitarianism.

George Orwell—www.biography.com/people/george-orwell-9429833
Learn more with this biography of George Orwell.

Timeline—www.historyguide.org/europe/orwell.html
This page features a timeline of the major events of Orwell's life.

INDEX